W9-ANQ-671

Taking Your Camera to
PANAMA

Ted Park

Raintree Steck-Vaughn Publishers
A Harcourt Company

Austin · New York
www.steck-vaughn.com

Published by Raintree Steck-Vaughn Publishers,
an imprint of Steck-Vaughn Company

Library of Congress Cataloging-in-Publication Data
Park, Ted
     Panama / by Ted Park
       p. cm. — (Taking your camera to)
     Includes index.
     ISBN 0-7398-1808-2
     1. Panama—Juvenile literature. [1. Panama.] I. Title. II. Series.

F1563.2 .P37 2000
972.87—dc21   00-041310

Printed in the United States of America
10 9 8 7 6 5 4 3 2 1 LB 02 01 00

Photo acknowledgments
Cover ©Al Michaud/FPG International; pp.1, 3a ©Corbis; p.3b ©Michaud, Al/FPG International; p.3c ©Buddy Mays/FPG International; p.3d ©Superstock; p.4 ©Corbis; p.5 ©Lloyd, Harvey/FPG International; pp.8, 9 ©Corbis; p.11 ©Michaud, Al/FPG International; p.13 ©Corbis; p.15 ©Gail Shumway/FPG International; pp.16, 17, 19 ©Superstock; p.20 ©Corbis; p.21 ©Superstock; p.23 ©Buddy Mays/FPG International; pp.24a, 24b ©Corbis; p.25 ©Tomas van Houtryve/AP/Wide World, Inc.; p.27 ©Superstock; p.28a ©Lloyd, Harvey/FPG International; p.28b ©Superstock; p.29a ©Corbis; p.29b ©Buddy Mays/FPG International.

All statistics in the Quick Facts section come from *The New York Times Almanac* (2000) and *The World Almanac* (2000)

Contents

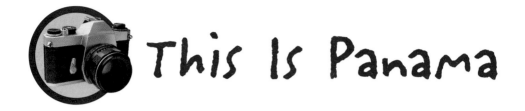 This Is Panama

Panama is a small country in Central America. It has mountains and jungles. There are also sandy beaches. If you took your camera to Panama, you could photograph many things.

You might see big farms where farmers grow bananas. And nearby there may be rain forests.

Panama has only a few large cities. One of them is Panama City, the capital.

Crocodiles sleep along Panama's riverbanks.

Skyscrapers in Panama City

One of the most famous places in the country is the Panama Canal. A canal is a waterway dug across land.

This book will show you many of these places. It will also tell you much about Panama. By knowing about the country before you take your camera there, you will enjoy your visit more.

 # The Place

The country of Panama is a land bridge between Central America and South America. A land bridge is a strip of land that connects two larger areas of land. Costa Rica borders Panama on the west. Colombia, in South America, borders it on the east. To the north is the Caribbean Sea, and to the south is the Pacific Ocean. Panama is 30,193 square miles (78,200 sq km). This makes it slightly smaller than the state of South Carolina.

The part of the Atlantic Ocean that is near Panama is known as the Caribbean Sea. The coastline of Panama that borders the Caribbean Sea is 477 miles (768 km) long. Panama's Pacific coastline is 767 miles (1,234 km) long. At Panama's narrowest point, only 50 miles (80 km) of land separate the Atlantic Ocean from the Pacific Ocean.

Mountains run the length of Panama. Much of the country is rocky. Forests cover about half of the country. The wood of the mahogany tree is one of Panama's biggest exports. But when a tree is cut down, soil may wash away.

 6

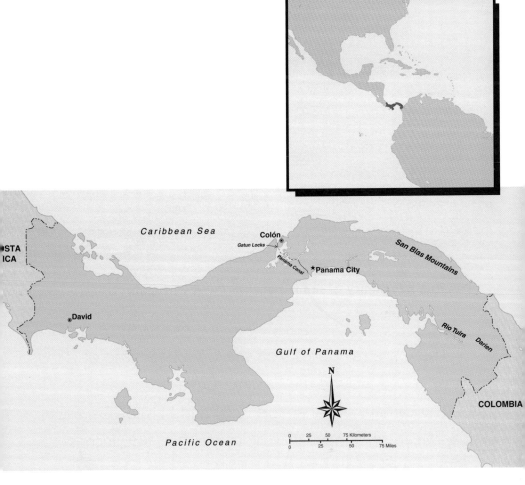

Caribbean Sea

COSTA
RICA

Colón

Gatun Locks

Panama Canal

★Panama City

San Blas Mountains

David

Río Tuira

Darién

Gulf of Panama

COLOMBIA

N

0   25   50   75 Kilometers
0   25   50   75 Miles

Pacific Ocean

7 📷

Panama has plenty of sandy beaches lined with palm trees.

There are rain forests on the Caribbean side of Panama and around the Panama Canal.

The climate of Panama is rainy and humid. On the Caribbean side, there may be as much as 130 inches (325 cm) of rain each year. There is much less rainfall on the Pacific Ocean side of the country. The dry season is from December through April. The weather is cooler in the mountains.

Panama has about 500 rivers, but they are small and it is hard to sail boats on them. More than 1,500 islands are off the Pacific coast.

 8

Panama also has an unexplored area that covers about one fifth of the country. It is called the Darién, and it is in the east. The Darién is one of the wettest places in the world. There are no towns and only one road there.

The Kuna and Chocó Indians live there. There are also descendants of Africans who live in the Darién.

More than three fifths of Panama is rolling hills.

The Panama Canal

The Panama Canal connects the Atlantic and Pacific oceans. It was built in 1914. Before the canal was built, ships had to sail around Cape Horn at the southern end of South America to get from one ocean to the other. Now they sail through the canal.

The canal is a combination of lakes and locks that ships sail through. A lock is an area with gates at each end. The gates allow the locks to fill with water. Ships sail into the locks and the rising water lifts them up through the mountains. The Gatun Locks on the Atlantic side of the canal are 110 feet (33.5 m) wide, 1,000 feet (304.8 m) long, and 81 feet (24.7 m) high.

Since the Panama Canal was finished, more than 800,000 ships have crossed the canal. Today about a thousand ships a month sail through it.

It takes a ship about 15 hours to travel through the canal. It is 50 miles (80-km) long.

 10

 # Places to Visit

The capital of Panama was first built in 1519. Much of it was destroyed, and the new city was built 7 miles (11 km) away. Panama City is one of the richest cities in Central America. If you took your camera to Panama City, you could take photographs of many things. One part of the city has narrow streets lined with buildings from the late 1600s. In another part there are tall, modern buildings. Panama City also has many beautiful parks and a walkway that is next to the sea.

From several mountains in Panama you can see the Pacific Ocean on one side. Then you can turn around and see the Atlantic Ocean. This happens in no other place in the world.

The Pearl Islands are a group of islands in the Gulf of Panama. They are famous for their oyster beds and the pearls that come from the oysters.

The Pearl Islands are a group of about 90 islands.

 12

The People

Almost 3 million people live in Panama today. About three fourths of them are mestizos. At one time this meant that most Panamanian mestizos had one ancestor who was Spanish and one who was a native Indian. Today, the meaning is different. Panamanian mestizos can be a mix of almost any peoples. Some West Indians also live in Panama. There are many blacks and mulattos who live in Panama. Mulattos are people with both African and European ancestors.

Indians also live in Panama. There are five known tribes in Panama, of whom the Guaymis have the largest number of people. There are about 125,000 Guaymis in Panama. Another well-known tribe are the Kuna. The Kuna keep many of their old traditions.

The Kuna Indians live in the Darién and on the islands along Panama's western coast.

The official language of Panama is Spanish. Many people also speak English. Many Indians do not speak Spanish. They have their own languages. Indians with some Spanish ancestors are called Ladinos. They usually adopt western-style dress and culture.

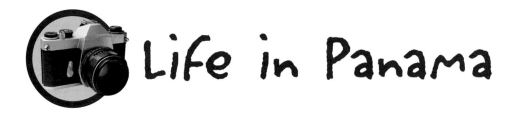# Life in Panama

Family life is important to the Panamanians, especially those who live in rural areas. Many relatives may live together, or close to one another. They especially like to celebrate holidays together.

Many of these family groups are breaking up. This is because many Panamanians are moving to cities to look for work. This is true of young people especially.

A native Indian from the Darién carving a canoe paddle.

Dyeing reeds

About one third of Panama's people are under the age of 15.

In the cities, wealthy people may live in apartments. Poor people may live nearby, in poor sections.

Government and Religion

Panama was part of Colombia until 1903. Today it is a constitutional republic. This means that its citizens elect the president, or person who leads the country. The leader follows a constitution, or a plan of government. The president is elected for five years. He or she is assisted by two elected vice presidents and a group of advisers. The Legislative Assembly makes the country's laws. Members are elected for five years.

Most people in Panama are Roman Catholic. Most church services are well attended, and churches are kept open all day long. In Panama City there is a famous church. It has a large altar made of gold.

The Church of the Virgin of the Carmine

Earning a Living

The chief crops of Panama are bananas, sugar, and coffee. Only about one fourth of the land can be farmed. This means that most of the food must be imported, or brought in, from other countries.

About 10,000 people work in the Canal Zone, a strip of land 10 miles (16 km) wide. It runs north to south on each side of the Panama Canal.

Panama does not have many natural resources. These are materials from nature that are useful to people.

About one third of the Panamanian people are farmers.

Gathering bananas

Because of this, the country has to import the natural resources it needs to make manufactured goods. Copper is the most important resource that is mined, or dug from the earth. Miners also dig limestone, clay, and sea salt.

Panama's fishing industry is very important. Bananas are Panama's biggest export, or things shipped out of the country to be sold. Shellfish are the second largest export. Chicken farms are a new industry in Panama. Banking and tourism are also growing industries.

School and Sports

Children must go to school from ages 6 to 15. Many schools are public, but some are run by the Catholic church. In many rural areas, there are no schools. Many children there have to help their families work on their farms. A student must go to school for 12 years in order to attend a university. Panama has three universities. The largest is the University of Panama, which has 32,000 students.

Soccer has recently become the national sport. Swimming and diving are also popular. And many people like to go deep-sea fishing and snorkeling as well. Panamanians enjoy horse racing, volleyball, cycling, and hiking. People in Panama also like baseball, softball, and basketball. Panama has more than 940 kinds of birds. Because of this, bird watching is popular.

Because there is so much water around Panama, outdoor activities such as sailing are popular.

Food and Holidays

Most Panamanians eat a great deal of corn, rice, and beans. They also eat tortillas, which are flat breads made from cornmeal. These are filled with meat, beans, and cheese. Black beans are popular in Panama.

A popular Panamanian dish is ceviche. This is made of raw fish or shellfish that has been soaked in lime or lemon juice, olive oil and hot spices. Panamanians like their food spicy.

Tamales are made of corn dough. They are filled, wrapped in a banana leaf, and steamed.

This boy is selling candied apples during a carnival that is held before Lent.

Panama City has a famous carnival each year. It takes place in March or April. The carnival lasts for four days and ends when Lent begins. Costumes, music, dancing, and parades are part of this carnival.

The most important holidays in Panama are religious ones. Holy Week, Easter, and Christmas are some of the holidays the people of Panama celebrate. On Good Friday, there are processions around the church. In farming areas, fiestas, or festivals, take place.

 # The Future

If you took your camera to Panama, you could take pictures of a country that is changing. Many new things are happening there. Education and health care have improved. People are now expected to live longer. Tourism is growing and brings money into the country.

The Trans-Panama Oil Pipeline is an important part of the future. It brings oil to the Pacific shore and then sends it underground to the Atlantic side. Ships used to carry most of this oil through the Panama Canal.

Like many countries, Panama does have problems. Because the country has to import so much food and goods, it is not a wealthy country. Although Panama is one of the richest Central American countries, many people are still poor and may not have enough to eat.

The people of Panama want to solve their problems. They look to the future with excitement. When you leave Panama, people may say *"Hasta luego"* to you. These Spanish words mean "See you later."

The fishing industry helps bring money into Panama.

Quick Facts About
PANAMA

Capital
Panama City

Borders
Colombia, Costa Rica

Area
30,193 square miles
(78,200 sq km)

Population
2.7 million

Largest cities
Panama City (625,150 people);
Colón (137,825 people);
David (99,811 people)

Chief crops
Bananas, rice, sugarcane, coffee,
corn

Natural resources
Copper, mahogany forests, shrimp

Longest river
Tuira, at 125 miles (201 km)

28

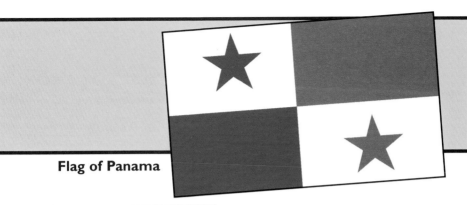

Flag of Panama

Coastline
1,546 miles (2,490 km)

Monetary unit
balboa

Literacy rate
91 percent of the Panamanians can read and write.

Major industries
Manufacturing, construction, oil refining, cement

29

Glossary

canal A waterway dug across land

Canal Zone A strip of land that runs north to south on each side of the Panama Canal

ceviche (suh-VEE-chay) A dish made of raw fish or shellfish that is soaked in lime or lemon juice and seasoned with hot spice

Darién (dar-ee-EN) A wet, unexplored area in the eastern half of Panama

exports Goods shipped out of a country to be sold

Guaymis Indians (gweye-MIS) The largest of the native Panamanian Indian tribes

imports Goods brought into a country

Kuna Indians (KO-nuh) A well-known tribe of native Panamanian Indians

Ladinos (luh-DEE-noz) Native Panamanian Indians who adopt western dress and culture

land bridge A strip of land that connects two larger areas of land

lock An area with gates at either end that fills with water, raising and lowering ships so they can travel through countrysides of different heights

mestizos (meh-STEE-zos) At one time, a person with one Spanish and one native Indian ancestor. Today, the ancestors can be a mix of almost any peoples.

mulattos (muh-LAH-toz) People with both African and European ancestors

natural resources Materials from nature that are useful to people

Panama Canal A passageway through Panama that allows ships to go between the Atlantic and Pacific oceans without sailing around South America

Panama City The capital of Panama

Pearl Islands A group of about 90 islands in the Gulf of Panama famous for their oyster beds and pearls

rain forest A place where the trees are very tall and close together and many plants and animals live

tamales (tuh-MAH-leez) A popular dish made of cornmeal dough that is filled with meat, wrapped in a banana leaf, and steamed

tortillas (tor-TEE-yuhz) Flat breads made from cornmeal

Index